Squirrels

Emily Rose Townsend
AR B.L.: 1.6
Points: 0.5

LG

Woodland Animals

Squirrels

gray squirrel

by Emily Rose Townsend

Consulting Editor: Gail Saunders-Smith, Ph.D.

Consultant: William John Ripple, Professor
Department of Forest Resources
Oregon State University

Capstone
press

Mankato, Minnesota

Pebble Books are published by Capstone Press
151 Good Counsel Drive, P.O. Box 669, Mankato, Minnesota 56002
www.capstonepress.com

1 2 3 4 5 6 09 08 07 06 05 04

Library of Congress Cataloging-in-Publication Data
    Townsend, Emily Rose.
    Squirrels / by Emily Rose Townsend.
    p. cm.—(Woodland animals)
    Includes bibliographical references (p. 23) and index.
    Contents: Squirrels—What squirrels do—Day and night.
    ISBN-13: 978-0-7368-2069-1 (hardcover)
    ISBN-10: 0-7368-2069-8 (hardcover)
1. Squirrels—Juvenile literature. [1. Squirrels.] I. Title.
QL737.R68T68 2004
599.36—dc 21   2003011186

Note to Parents and Teachers

The Woodland Animals series supports national science standards related to life science. This book describes and illustrates squirrels that live in woodlands. The photographs support early readers in understanding the text. The repetition of words and phrases helps early readers learn new words. This book also introduces early readers to subject-specific vocabulary words, which are defined in the Glossary. Early readers may need assistance to read some words and to use the Table of Contents, Glossary, Read More, Internet Sites, and Index/Word List sections of the book.

Table of Contents

Squirrels

Squirrels are rodents
with long, bushy tails.
Squirrels have sharp claws.

gray squirrel

Many squirrels climb trees.
Squirrels use their tails
to balance.

red squirrel

Squirrels have red, brown, gray, black, or white fur.

red squirrel

areas where squirrels live

Many squirrels live in woodlands. Woodlands are covered with trees and shrubs.

Some squirrels dig burrows. Other squirrels build nests in trees.

Uinta ground squirrel

What Squirrels Do

Some squirrels glide between trees. They look like they are flying. These squirrels are called flying squirrels.

Southern flying squirrel

Squirrels eat nuts,
seeds, plants, and insects.

Squirrels put food in their cheek pouches.

golden-mantled ground squirrel

Day and Night

Squirrels often look for food during the day. They sleep at night.

red squirrel

Glossary

balance—to keep steady and not fall

burrow—a hole or tunnel in the ground made by an animal

claw—a hard, curved nail on the feet of some animals; many squirrels use their sharp claws to climb trees.

glide—to move smoothly and easily

pouch—a part of a squirrel's mouth that is like a pocket; squirrels use their pouches to carry food to their burrow or nest to store.

rodent—a small mammal with long front teeth used for gnawing; a squirrel is a rodent; squirrels eat nuts, seeds, plants, insects, and very small animals.

shrub—a plant or bush with woody stems that branch out near the ground

woodland—land that is covered by trees and shrubs; woodlands are also called forests.

Read More

Olien, Rebecca. *Squirrels: Furry Scurriers.*
The Wild World of Animals. Mankato, Minn.:
Bridgestone Books, 2002.

Swanson, Diane. *Squirrels.* Welcome to the
World of Animals. Milwaukee: Gareth Stevens,
2003.

Internet Sites

FactHound offers a safe, fun way to find Internet sites
related to this book. All of the sites on FactHound
have been researched by our staff.

Here's how:

1. Visit *www.facthound.com*

2. Type in this special code **0736820698** for
   age-appropriate sites. Or enter a search word
   related to this book for a more general search.

3. Click on the **Fetch It** button.

FactHound will fetch the best sites for you!

23

Index/Word List

Word Count: 95
Early-Intervention Level: 13

Editorial Credits

Mari C. Schuh, editor; Patrick D. Dentinger, designer; Scott Thoms, photo researcher;
   Karen Risch, product planning editor

Photo Credits

Ann & Rob Simpson, 1
Comstock, 10
Corbis/Joe McDonald, 14; Wolfgang Kaehler, 12
Corel, 16
Digital Stock, cover
Getty Images/Time Life Pictures/Brian Miller/Ovoworks, 6
Kent & Donna Dannen, 18
Tom Stack & Associates/Joe McDonald, 4; John Gerlach, 8; Thomas Kitchin, 20

24